LEO THE LION

TANNER DI BELLA

XULON PRESS

Xulon Press
2301 Lucien Way #415
Maitland, FL 32751
407.339.4217
www.xulonpress.com

Paperback ISBN-13: 978-1-66287-321-8
Hard Cover ISBN-13: 978-1-66287-401-7

It was a beautiful day in the jungle
Where Leo wanted to play.
He found his forest friends
And he had something to say.

"Let's go run and play," he said,
"And race to the farthest tree."
Ready, set, go they went —
Dashed off wild and free.

1

But Leo's friends were faster;
He began to fall behind.
He couldn't keep up with them,
No matter how hard he tried.

"If I can't run fast like them, " he thought,

"I might be someone else.

Maybe I am not a lion.

Maybe I'm not even myself."

So, he went and found his feathered
Friend so high up in the sky.
"Hello there!" he yelled to him,
"Let's see if I can fly."

6

He ran to the tallest rock,
And began to jump with glee,
Thinking, "Surely, this is who I am.
You just wait and see."

But, Leo landed with a thump
Right there on the ground.
He began to sit and slump.
Then he heard a sound...

Overhead, his monkey friend
Was swinging through the trees.
"Ah ha," Leo said with pride,
"This should be a breeze!"

"I can surely swing like that,
This is who I'm made to be.
I will live up high like a
Monkey in the trees!"

He climbed to the tallest branch,
Hanging from his bushy tail.
"Oo oo ah ah," he said aloud,
But he began to flail.

He tumbled down so very far
And landed with a splash.
"I guess that's not who I am."
His patience was wearing fast.

"Perhaps I am a fish like them
And I'm meant to swim all day!"
But, Leo couldn't hold his breath,
So he could no longer stay.

Then Leo began to cry,
"I don't know who to be.
I don't fit in with anyone.
I don't even feel like me..."

Leo's father heard him cry,
And wondered what was wrong.
He wrapped him in his arms,
And held him there so strong.

"I don't know who I am.

I'm not like all the rest."

"Of course, you're not," his father said,

"You were made to be the best."

25

"You're not Leo the monkey

Or Leo the fish or Leo the flying bird.

You are Leo the Magnificent Lion,

And a part of our family herd."

"Just because you can't run fast
Does not change who you are.
You're a lion no a matter what.
I think you're the best Leo by far."

28

"God made you in His eyes.
You're precious in His sight.
You're his most prized creation.
You're Leo the Lion, that's right!"

"If you ever feel confused again, Leo,
And forget what's really true,
God is just a prayer away.
He's always there for you."

CPSIA information can be obtained
at www.ICGtesting.com
Printed in the USA
BVHW011306200623
666146BV00017B/353